TIRED OF EATING PEANUT BUTTER AND JELLY SANDWICHES?

Tips to Get a Job Fast!!

JAMES WATSON PH.D.

Disclaimer:
Every effort has been made to make this book as complete and as accurate as possible. However, there may be mistakes, both typographical and in content. Therefore, this text should be used only as a general guide and not as the ultimate source of information. The purpose of this book is to educate. The author shall have neither liability nor responsibility to any person or entity with respect to any loss or damage caused, or alleged to have been caused, directly or indirectly, by the information contained in this book.
Copyright © 2014 James Watson
All rights reserved.

ISBN: 1501059971
ISBN 13: 9781501059971
Library of Congress Control Number: 2014916049
CreateSpace Independent Publishing Platform
North Charleston, South Carolina

TIRED OF EATING PEANUT BUTTER AND JELLY SANDWICHES?

Tips to Get a Job Fast!!

JAMES WATSON PH.D.

Contents

Acknowledgments · vii
Preface · ix
Chapter 1   The Harsh Realities of Today's Job Market · · · · · · · · · · · · · · 1
Chapter 2   Your Toolbox · 11
              A. Your Twenty-Second Answer to
              "Why Were You Laid Off?" · 12
              B. Your Thirty-Second Elevator Speech · · · · · · · · · · · · · · · · · 13
              C. Your Network · 14
              D. Your Business Card · 21
              E. LinkedIn · 23
Chapter 3   Your Résumé · 25
              A. Ground Rules · 25
              B. Heading · 29
              C. Summary · 30
              D. Core Competencies · 38
              E. Professional Experience · 41
              F. Education · 56
              G. Certifications and Security Clearances · · · · · · · · · · · · · · · 57
              H. Military Service · 58
              I. Sample Résumé · 59
              J. Miscellaneous · 63
Chapter 4   Cover Letter · 68
Chapter 5   Interviewing · 73
Chapter 6   Miscellaneous Tips · 94
About the Author · 101

Acknowledgments

My acknowledgments come in two parts.

First, as a hiring manager: In the earlier days at General Atomics, I was the director of the Materials and Chemistry Division, a group of about 120 technical experts and technicians. In this role, I interviewed hundreds of candidates for technical positions throughout the company and made the final hiring decisions for those in my division. I am pleased to acknowledge the assistance I received from individuals in the human relations department, especially Art Stoddard and Hank Anthony.

Second, as a job seeker: I am pleased to acknowledge the help and insights I received from Bob Trevithick, the first vice president of human relations at General Atomics, and John DeWitt and Fred Dawn of Lee Hecht Harrison. I am also pleased to acknowledge the assistance of Grace Decker, founder and director of the Boardroom San Diego, and the many speakers she scheduled for presentations at the Boardroom. Two of these speakers who influenced my thinking were Carl Wellenstein and Phil Blair. I am also indebted to the many individuals who came to the Boardroom for assistance with their job searches and shared their job-seeking experiences with me.

Preface

The following pages are intended for those who have decided on a career and are ready to begin their job search. Those who have not yet decided on a career path are referred to excellent books on how to find your life calling, such as *What Color Is Your Parachute?* by Nelson Bolles and *Job Won* by Phil Blair. Do not begin your search until you know what you want to do with the rest of the working part of your life.

1

THE HARSH REALITIES OF TODAY'S JOB MARKET

The following are some of the harsh realities job seekers face in today's market:

- Jobs are scarce, and unemployment is high.

- Employers are delaying hiring because of unsettled times.

- Only about 15 percent of jobs are ever advertised.

- The other almost 85 percent are in the "hidden" job market. The *only* way to find these hidden jobs is by networking (more on networking later).

TIRED OF EATING PEANUT BUTTER AND JELLY SANDWICHES?

- Job advertisements may be false. Companies may use false advertisements to:

    - meet legal requirements when they have already chosen the candidate they want;

    - see if their own employees are looking; or

    - gauge the market.

The Harsh Realities of Today's Job Market

- Another fib: "We aren't hiring right now," or "We have a job freeze." The truth is companies are *always* hiring.

- Companies hate to advertise their job openings; it is their last resort.

- Their first choice is referrals from trusted sources, i.e., networking.

The Harsh Realities of Today's Job Market

- Many companies' HR departments are overwhelmed with job applications and are shorthanded.

- As a result, many applications go unanswered. So don't be surprised if you never hear back (the "black hole" of information).

TIRED OF EATING PEANUT BUTTER AND JELLY SANDWICHES?

- Discrimination is still rampant on several fronts, including:
  - age
  - sex
  - race

The Harsh Realities of Today's Job Market

- Many people are embarrassed to tell their friends and family they have lost their job. You must get over this.

- "All jobs are temporary."—Anonymous

- Currently, the average job duration is one and a half to two years.

- Hundreds of people are laid off every day.

- Major League ball players aren't surprised when they strike out; it's part of the game.

Tired of Eating Peanut Butter and Jelly Sandwiches?

Remember that recruiting agencies work for their clients, not for you.
- Working through an agency is a low-probability effort (less than 15 percent), while networking yields about 85 percent of jobs, so divide your time accordingly.

The Harsh Realities of Today's Job Market

- However, some people find success by getting a temporary job via an agency and then working it into a permanent job through outstanding performance as a temp.

Tired of Eating Peanut Butter and Jelly Sandwiches?

- You should not spend more than 10 percent of your time sitting at your computer answering job advertisements. Most of this effort is a waste of time.

- You *must* get out of the house, meet people, form your network, and work it every day.

2

Your Toolbox

The following tools should be in your job-search toolbox:

1. Your twenty-second answer to "Why were you laid off?"

2. Your thirty-second elevator speech

3. Your network

4. Your résumé and cover letter

5. LinkedIn

6. Your business card

A. Your Twenty-Second Answer to "Why Were You Laid Off?"

- Give it a positive spin, such as:

    - "The company changed direction, and my skills became less important."

    - "My company's customer requirements changed, and my specialties were no longer needed."

- End on an upbeat note, such as:

    - "Now I'm looking for a position that is a better fit for my skill set."

    - "Now I'm looking for a position that contributes directly to the bottom line."

- Practice it over and over until it is automatic.

- Don't act or sound embarrassed; hundreds of people are laid off every day.

B. Your Thirty-Second Elevator Speech

- Have a thirty-second "elevator speech" ready at all times (a typical elevator ride lasts thirty seconds). The speech should include the following information:

  - who you are

  - what you are good at

  - what job you are looking for

- *Don't ramble.*

- Practice it over and over until it is automatic.

C. Your Network

- Networking means:

    - contacting all acquaintances you have—no matter how distant—and telling them you are looking for a certain type of job

    - asking them to tell their friends

    - being active and making new friends in your field

    - joining clubs and professional societies in your field

    - participating in organizations like Toastmasters and the Boardroom

Your Toolbox

- You will find that some people you thought were close friends won't find the time to help you, while other distant acquaintances will lean over backward to help you.

- So, contact *all* family, friends, and acquaintances, no matter how distant or remote.

- Be visible. Do those things that make your name come up on social media.

    - Join related clubs and societies—participate, become a club officer.

    - Give talks about your field.

    - Publish articles and papers.

    - Join a Toastmasters club.

Your Toolbox

- An out-of-the-box idea that has worked for some people is to ask your doctor, dentist, lawyer, minister, priest, rabbi, tax preparer, broker, etc. (anyone who provides you with professional services and has a mailing list) if he or she will forward your résumé to all of his or her clients with a favorable recommendation.

(*Thanks to Linda Melikian for this suggestion.)

TIRED OF EATING PEANUT BUTTER AND JELLY SANDWICHES?

- The following are helpful locations where you can attend meetings and create contacts:

    - CONNECT.org

    - meetingandmixers.com

    - freshnews.com

    - volunteersandiego.org

    - COMMNEXUS

    - BIOCOM

    - CleanTECH

    - Toastmasters

Your Toolbox

- It isn't "who you know."

- It isn't "what you know."

- It's who knows you and whether they will go to bat for you.

- Reality check: enter your name on a search engine or on social media sites and see what comes up.

- If you don't appear, get busy with the ideas in this book and others.

Your Toolbox

D. Your Business Card

- Have your business card ready to hand out at all times!

Tired of Eating Peanut Butter and Jelly Sandwiches?

- On the front side:

    - state your primary capability

    - no picture of you

    - make yourself easy to contact

- Include the following:

    - home phone

    - cell phone

    - e-mail address

    - LinkedIn address

- Do not include your home address.

- On the back side:

    - details of your capabilities in bullets

E. LinkedIn

- Your LinkedIn page is an extremely important part of your toolbox; join it at: https://www.linkedin.com/reg/join.

- Become an expert by attending a lecture or reading a book; there is far more to it than can be covered here.

- In the description of yourself, sprinkle in and repeat words that describe your skills, talents, and interests.

- Get a professional picture—smile!

- LinkedIn allows you to find people who work at the company you are interested in.

- Review this list to see if you have any connections to any of these individuals.

- Use these connections to gain information about the company and introductions with employees.

3

Your Résumé

A. Ground Rules

- Create a new job-specific résumé for every new job opportunity.

- Tailor it to the requirements of that specific job.

- Don't even think of one-size-fits-all!

- Scan job openings for key words, and use them frequently in all parts of your résumé.

- Key words are the descriptive words that are used in the job advertisement.

Your Résumé

- In many companies, the first thing that happens is your résumé is read by a computer for their key words (words they used in their advertisement).

- Sprinkle these key words throughout your résumé. Otherwise, you won't even survive this first screening step.

- There are many ways to write résumés. The one that follows is my favorite.

- To review other types, refer to books such as *What Color Is Your Parachute?* by Nelson Boles, *12 Steps to a New Career* by Carl Wellenstein, or *Job Won* by Phil Blair.

Your Résumé

B. Heading

- First is your heading:

    - name

    - home phone

    - cell phone

    - e-mail address

    - LinkedIn address

    - no home address

Example:

JOHN C. TAYLOR, PMP

Home: xxx-xxx-xxxx   jctaylor45@gmail.com
Cell: xxx-xxx-xxxx   LinkedIn: www.linkedin.com/in/xxxxxxx

C. Summary

- Then, your summary:

    - Have the first sentence in your summary clearly state what *one* job you are seeking.

    - Don't say you are looking for more than one job.

Your Résumé

- If you are interested in—and qualified for—more than one job, prepare a separate résumé for each one.

- Hiring managers are only trying to fill one position.

- Don't make the hiring manager have to figure out which job you are looking for—he or she won't (instead, he or she will throw your résumé into the trash and quickly move on to the next résumé in the pile).

Your Résumé

- You only get five to ten seconds before the reader decides either to read further or throw your résumé in the trash.

- This means that you must immediately give him or her several of your best achievements to grab his or her attention ("grabbers") and cause him or her to read further.

- The "grabbers" are examples of good things you made happen in jobs you have had, using measureable achievements like:

    - increased profit (X%)

    - reduced cost (Y%)

    - time saved (Z days) in cycle time

    - completing the same job with fewer people

Your Résumé

- Use action verbs like:

    achieved
    broadened
    constructed
    designed

(*Go to Google for more than one hundred examples.)

Tired of Eating Peanut Butter and Jelly Sandwiches?

- If you don't grab the reader's attention in the summary, your résumé goes into the trash—no matter how good the rest of it is.

- *Don't use buzzwords.*

  - examples: *fast-paced, dynamic, team player,* etc.

  - They are meaningless because they aren't backed up by any facts.

- Instead, say what you achieved.

Summary example:

SUMMARY

Life sciences marketing expert seeking position as vice president of business development in San Jose. Championed robotic surgery system evaluation in ten hospitals for thirty-seven procedures with twelve surgeons that increased revenues $9M per year. Led $450MM revenue growth 8 to 10 percent year over year. Grew sales on specialty pump franchise from $12MM to $22MM annually in two years.

Or for a person returning to the workplace after some time away:

MBA with experience in finance, audit, and fundraising returning to the workforce after twelve years as a homemaker, seeking position as a financial advisor in the San Juan Capistrano area. During time away from the business world, led fundraising budgets for six school sites with revenue exceeding $900K. Also introduced marketing and communication strategies that generated over $385K in donations to support technology, science, art, and physical education programs.

D. Core Competencies

- List no more than three.

- Hiring managers don't believe anyone is an expert in more than three.

- If the job description requires specific core competencies, include them or some close variation.

- Example:

CORE COMPETENCIES

- product life cycle management

- FDA approval and ISO compliance

- e-marketing, social media, web analytics

TIRED OF EATING PEANUT BUTTER AND JELLY SANDWICHES?

Next, *professional experience…*

E. Professional Experience

- The hiring manager will have at least fifty to a hundred other résumés to review, and many of them will appear to be as good as yours. This means you *must* put your best stuff up front. Otherwise, your résumé goes into the trash.

- For each former position (most recent first) include:

  - first line: name of company and dates (month and year) of employment

  - second line: brief description of the company

  - third line: your position

  - specific examples of what you achieved in this position—do not say "responsible for" or "managed."

Your Résumé

- Don't leave any blank periods of time.

- If you have been out of the workforce (e.g., to raise a family), say what constructive things you did during that time (e.g., volunteered with the Salvation Army).

TIRED OF EATING PEANUT BUTTER AND JELLY SANDWICHES?

- If you are unemployed, call yourself a "consultant" for the period of time from the end of your last job up to "present" and say what constructive things you did during this time, such as "learned to speak Spanish" or "volunteered at the Red Cross."

Your Résumé

- The chance that your summary will be read is about 80 percent; if it is a grabber, the chance that your core competencies will be read is about 50 percent and then first professional experience is about 25 percent, and the rest of the professional experience section and everything else is below 2 percent.

- This means you should give most of your professional experience space to your most recent job.

- Don't go back more than ten years on your professional experience. Professional experience older than ten years is viewed as irrelevant.

Your Résumé

- I recommend limiting your résumé to one page because the chance of the second or third page being read is close to zero.

- Thus, the good stuff on pages two and three will never be read.

- Many senior and experienced candidates condense everything into one page. *Exception: there is no page limit on academic jobs.*

- I know it will be painful for you to delete all of the good stuff on your second (and even third) page, but remember, the purpose of the résumé is just to get an interview—not to tell the reader everything you have ever done.

- There will be time to go into these details from the second and third pages during the interview.

Your Résumé

- All of this advice leads to this question: "How do I make my résumé stand out from all the others that also appear to be very good?"

- The answer is to have one or two outstanding achievements for every previous position. (For example, what good thing did you make happen while you were in this assignment?)

- Put the most emphasis on the most recent positions.

TIRED OF EATING PEANUT BUTTER AND JELLY SANDWICHES?

- Use action verbs, like:

    achieved
    broadened
    constructed
    designed

(*Go to Google for more action verbs.)

Your Résumé

- Do not say "responsible for" or "managed." These words can make a list of experience items come across as a boring laundry list.

- Why would I want to hire you instead of all these other people who have what appears to be comparable experience?

- The answer is your outstanding achievements in your previous positions.

Examples of professional experience:

PROFESSIONAL EXPERIENCE

Resolute Research, San Diego, CA   **Dec. 2005–Present**

A professional services company engaged in project management and financial analysis

Director Project Management
- Initiated project charter and acquired team to implement company infrastructure; resulting in establishment of banking, brokerages, contracts, training, and incorporation with a C-Corp and LLC.

- Applied fundamental analyses with industry and competitor research, financials, economic trends, and comparative key performance indicators; resulting in comprehensive DCF valuations.

- Trained and mentored experienced project managers with PMI-SD as instructor reporting to Vice President Professional Development and budget director reporting to Vice President Finance.

Biogen IDEC, San Diego, CA   **Sep. 2000–Nov. 2005**

A $2.4B biotechnology company

Senior Program Manager
- Restructured team to strategic core team and tactical subteams for technical and business functions, resulting in substantially improved critical discussions and meeting efficiency over 100 percent.

- Developed multiproject planning, integrating development programs with capacity constrained resources, resulting in revised project prioritization and portfolio management across nine programs.

- Appointed to Strategic Planning Advisory Committee, Portfolio Management Committee, Process Improvement Committee, Merger Integration Subteam, and Due Diligence Committee.

- Next, your *education*...

F. EDUCATION

- Include degree, field, and institution.

- Do not include the date of the degree.

Example of education:

EDUCATION

BS, Business Management, Cornell University
MBA, Finance, Stanford University

Continuing Education/Skills:
Six Sigma Green Belt, project management, diversity training, harassment training, production inventory control, Microsoft Office Suite, SAP.

G. Certifications and Security Clearances

Example of certifications and security clearances:

CERTIFICATIONS & SECURITY CLEARANCES

- CPA Certificate, November 1993—WA State License #16505
- Certified Treasury Professional, June 1991
- Accredited ACH Professional, October 2001
- Secret Security Clearance (Inactive)

Tired of Eating Peanut Butter and Jelly Sandwiches?

H. Military Service

Last, list your *military service* (if any).

Example:

MILITARY SERVICE

US Army, Division Artillery field grade officer

I. Sample Résumé

Now, put it all together for a complete résumé.

Tired of Eating Peanut Butter and Jelly Sandwiches?

ROBERT T. JONES, PMP

Home: (xxx) xxx-xxxx　　　　　　　　　jonesak78@gmail.com
Cell: (xxx) xxx-xxxx　　　　　　　　　www.linkedin.com/in/jonesak78

SUMMARY

Manufacturing executive with experience in domestic and international markets seeking position in the Sunnyvale area. Grew revenue 25 percent over four-year period by developing standard product development procedures. Led a manufacturing strategy that vertically integrated key operations resulting in an 18 percent reduction in cost. Drove a metrics-driven culture resulting in 100 percent schedule adherence, 98 percent first pass yield rates, 2–3 percent yearly operational cost reduction and labor adherence of 99 percent.

CORE COMPETENCIES

- Product Line Transfer and Integration

- Resource, Inventory, and Space Optimization

- Quality Management System

Your Résumé

PROFESSIONAL EXPERIENCE

SANDERSON MEDICAL, INC., Sunnyvale, CA   1998–2014
Sanderson offers a complete line of hearing aids.
Director of Operations
- Managed the relocation of manufacturing, warehousing/distribution, and customer service from the United States to Mexico.

- Developed and administered separation packages for redundant positions.

- Led the implementation of a new Enterprise Resource Planning (ERP) platform that resulted in improved software reliability, sales order processing, financial reporting, and production forecasting and warehouse management.

- Worked with engineering, quality assurance, and regulatory affairs on releasing new products, developing new processes, and resolving day-to-day manufacturing issues.

Manager of Operations   2002–2006
- Managed the site selection, layout, and setup of the new site.

- Increased cycle count accuracy to 98.5 percent and reduced customer shipping errors to 0.05 percent by employing lean distribution and manufacturing practices.

EDUCATION AND PROFESSIONAL DEVELOPMENT

MBA, Finance, University of Michigan
BS, Business Management, Purdue University
Corporate Training: Six Sigma Certification (in-progress), cGMP, ISO 13485, APICS,
Lean Manufacturing Practices, Ethics, Leadership, Safety

J. Miscellaneous

- Do not include personal information (unless relevant):

    - no hobbies or sports

    - no family details

    - no religious affiliations

    - no political affiliations

Buzzwords

- Avoid meaningless buzzwords and phrases like:

    proven track record
    strategic
    innovative
    passionate
    intuitive
    high impact
    fast-paced
    team player
    extensive experience
    results-oriented
    dynamic
    problem solver

General rule: avoid any adjective that isn't backed up by an example.

Your Résumé

- Buzzwords are meaningless and annoying.
- Instead, say what you did.

TIRED OF EATING PEANUT BUTTER AND JELLY SANDWICHES?

References:
- Do not include them on your résumé.

- If asked, say they will be provided separately.

- Handpick them for the specific job.

- Give them a heads-up to expect a call.

Your Résumé

- *Make sure* your résumé matches your LinkedIn page and business card.

4

Cover Letter

- The cover letter differs from the résumé by saying how your skills and experience match *this specific job*.

- Show how you meet job requirements.

- Use examples—tell a story.

- Close by saying you want the job and asking when you can expect an answer.

Cover Letter

- Be enthusiastic. Say why you want to join *this specific* company.

- Show that you have researched the company and understand where you would fit in.

- Give examples of how your experience fits the job description.

- Again, use the key words within the job description in several places throughout your cover letter.

If appropriate, include:
- a table with two columns; the first column quotes the job requirements, and the second facing column describes how your experience meets those requirements.

- Added benefits:

  - This automatically repeats key words from the job description.

  - It ensures you have addressed all job requirements.

COVER LETTER

EXAMPLE

Sir/Madam—

I am responding to your advertisement for a technical proposal manager with experience in aerospace technology. I have been managing technical proposals for various aspects of aircraft, rockets, and satellite technology for the past eight years. I am especially interested in joining the Oxford Aerospace Corporation because of your outstanding reputation for supporting leading-edge technologies and for personnel training and advancement. My experience matches your requirements in the following areas:

Your requirement: Experience in the use of themes, discriminators, and ghosts in proposals.

My experience: I have used themes, discriminators, and ghosts in numerous winning aerospace proposals to NASA, the US Air Force, and DARPA.

Your requirement: Knowledge of thermal transfer and thermodynamics as applied to reentry problems.

My experience: I have led teams that designed complete reentry systems that were based on extensive thermodynamic analyses and heat transfer through composite materials.

I have exceptional abilities to work across all organizational levels to develop all necessary components of the proposal. In some cases, this has meant working in harmony with my counterparts in other companies to present the strongest possible combination of capabilities and value to the customer. My previous engineering experience enables me to work across technical and business development departments.

Tired of Eating Peanut Butter and Jelly Sandwiches?

I believe that I have all of the necessary qualifications to work effectively in the Proposal Development Section within your Space Division in Salt Lake City.

I look forward to meeting with you.

Sincerely,

Walter C. Brooks

5

Interviewing

A Typical Interview Day

- Human resources (HR) will usually interview you first and last, set the day's agenda, introduce you to company policies, and answer "housekeeping" questions (e.g., travel arrangements, etc.)

- The hiring manager (and one or two of his or her staff) will interview you next. After hearing his or her staff's opinions of you, *he or she will make the hiring decision.* HR will normally agree with his or her decision (exception: the hiring manager missed some flagrant problem).

- HR will usually complete the day, asking if you have any final questions.

The Hiring Manager

- Questions the hiring manager is trying to answer—the "3 C's":

    - Competence—Can you do the job?

    - Chemistry—Will you fit in?

    - Confidence—Do you project a tone of self-assurance?

Interviewing

Competence

Can You Do the Job?

- You must demonstrate complete command of the job requirements.

- For a technical job, make sure you are up-to-date on fundamental "hammer and saw" aspects of the technology.

- Tell them how you solved a tough technical problem.

- Mention your patents, technical innovations, or other proof of your expertise.

Chemistry

Will You Fit In?

- Many technical jobs require you to work with a variety of people; the hiring manager will wonder how you will get along with:

    - senior managers and technicians within his or her division

    - other technical groups in the company

    - prima donnas

    - customers

    - government regulators

    - subcontractors

Interviewing

Confidence

Do You Project a Tone of Self-Assurance?

- This is a subjective impression conveyed largely by your speaking style, eye contact, etc.

- Consider joining a Toastmasters club to improve this skill.

Tired of Eating Peanut Butter and Jelly Sandwiches?

The employer's questions:
- Why are you here?
- What can you do for me?
- Will you fit in?
- How much will it cost?

Your questions:
- What does the job involve?
- Do my skills match the job?
- How would we get along?
- Can I persuade you to hire me?

Interviewing

- The person interviewing you is likely to open the interview by saying, "Tell me about yourself."

- Have a two-minute answer ready, including:

    - your early life (fifteen seconds)

    - where you went to school (fifteen seconds)

    - where you have worked, with measureable results (sixty seconds)

    - what job you want now (thirty seconds)

- *Don't ramble.*

- Practice it over and over until it is automatic.

- Have an answer to the question: "Why did you leave your last position?"

- Cast your answer in a good light:

  - company emphasis shifted away from your expertise

  - promotion opportunities were blocked

  - new management had different priorities

- Practice it over and over until it is automatic.

Interviewing

- The person interviewing you is probably as nervous as you are.

- He or she is thinking, *I will look bad if I hire someone who turns out to be a misfit.*

- Don't badmouth your present or past employers.

- Have an answer to the question: "What is your greatest weakness?"

- State some problem, and show how you overcame it.

- The person interviewing you may have very limited interviewing skills.

- Be ready to help him or her out by taking charge of the interview.

- Describe your two greatest achievements.

Interviewing

- Check the location of the interview site and parking place the day before.

- Arrive a few minutes early, relaxed and confident.

Tired of Eating Peanut Butter and Jelly Sandwiches?

- Ask what you will be expected to achieve in your first six months.

Interviewing

Thank-you letters:
- Send thank-you letters immediately (via US mail, not e-mail).

- Send them no later than the next day.

- Have a model ready before the interview so you can write letters quickly.

- No duplicates—write a different letter for each person who interviewed you.

- Mention points that were important to the interviewer—show how your strengths match the job.

- Thank everyone you talked to, including secretaries.

Follow-Up

- In many cases, weeks will go by after your interview with no feedback from the company.

- I recommend contacting the senior person you interviewed every two weeks by e-mail to ask about the status of your application.

- Add an attachment with some article of interest to his or her company.

Compensation

Compensation may be part of interviewing.

The hiring decision comes in two separate steps:
1. First, do we want to hire this person?

2. If yes, then—and only then—what will it cost?

- This means you are not risking the job offer by negotiating compensation.

- Employers expect you to negotiate compensation.

- Know the average nationwide salary ranges for persons with your degree and years of experience. This information is available in almost any library.

TIRED OF EATING PEANUT BUTTER AND JELLY SANDWICHES?

Compensation is much more than salary. It may include:
- travel expenses, car allowance

- bonus

- equity, stock options

- accelerated reviews

- tuition for related courses

- 401(k)

Interviewing

- Try to have the interviewer mention the salary offer first.

- He or she is likely to say a range (e.g. $60,000 to $65,000).

- You say, "Sixty-five thousand would be acceptable."

- This is not always possible, so know the typical salary range for a person with your skills and years of experience; if you must, mention a number in the upper half of the range.

6
Miscellaneous Tips

Tips and Unusual Ideas That Have Worked for Some People

Miscellaneous Tips

- Send a cover letter and résumé addressed to the CEO via FedEx, saying which job you want (FedEx because you can be sure that it will be delivered to and signed for by someone in the CEO's office).

- What is likely to happen:

    - CEO's secretary signs for your letter and forwards it to HR.

    - As your letter arrives in HR, they notice that it came from the CEO's office.

    - It gets looked at, and you are more likely to get an answer.

- At least, you may avoid the "black hole" of silence. At best, you may get an interview.

TIRED OF EATING PEANUT BUTTER AND JELLY SANDWICHES?

- As a way of scoring higher on the computer search of your résumé for the company's key words, copy the company's job description, and then, with the font set on white (i.e., invisible), paste it onto the end of both your résumé and cover letter. The computer search will score the invisible key words (unless the company's HR department has installed an app to screen out these types of words).

Miscellaneous Tips

- Don't endanger your present job by letting your employer know you are looking outside.

- A job advertisement that lists ten to fifteen job requirements means the company doesn't really know what they are looking for. Answer with your best capabilities.

Miscellaneous Tips

Happy Job Hunting!

- Job searching is a fickle, capricious task involving some degree of luck; however, the luckiest people seem to be those who work the hardest.

Good luck!

About the Author

James F. Watson, PhD, PE, FASM, has twenty-five years of experience interviewing, hiring, supervising, and promoting professionals in the fields of science and engineering. He is a registered professional engineer in the state of California and a fellow of the American Society for Metals.

Dr. Watson worked for seven corporations, three start-ups, and one government lab for a total of forty-plus years in scientific, engineering, and business development positions.

*Professional Engineer

*Fellow, American Society for Metals

Dr. Jim Watson's Background

- **Previous Titles**
    - Vice President, Marketing

    - Director, Materials and Chemistry Division

    - Senior Technical Advisor

    - Manager, Materials and Processes

    - Manager, Business Development

    - Plant Manager

ABOUT THE AUTHOR

- **Practice Areas**
    - Chemistry

    - Biomaterials

    - Engineering

    - Medical Products

    - Energy

    - Metallurgy

www.ingramcontent.com/pod-product-compliance
Lightning Source LLC
Chambersburg PA
CBHW071226170526
45165CB00003B/1003